ALBRECHT DÜRER AND ME

ALBRECHT DÜRER AND ME

DAVID ZIEROTH

HARBOUR
PUBLISHING

1 2 3 4 5 — 18 17 16 15 14

Harbour Publishing Co. Ltd.
P.O. Box 219, Madeira Park, BC, V0N 2H0
www.harbourpublishing.com

Edited by Silas White
Cover design by Shed Simas
Text design by Carleton Wilson
Printed and bound in Canada

Canada Council for the Arts | Conseil des Arts du Canada

Harbour Publishing acknowledges financial support from the Government of Canada through the Canada Book Fund and the Canada Council for the Arts, and from the Province of British Columbia through the BC Arts Council and the Book Publishing Tax Credit.

Cataloguing data available from Library and Archives Canada
ISBN 978-1-55017-674-2 (paper)
ISBN 978-1-55017-675-9 (ebook)

For those who called me away, and for those who called me back

Table of Contents

dislocation

our common dust

A MOMENT OF MISSING BELLS

Nothing, above all, is comparable to the new life that a reflective person experiences when he observes a new country. Though I am still always myself, I believe I have changed to the very marrow of my bones.

– from *Italian Journey* by Johann Wolfgang von Goethe,
translated by W. H. Auden and Elizabeth Mayer

DISLOCATION

Viennese shoes

in Wien, even the homeless wear good shoes
or at least one bedraggled, bearded, filthy-
coated giant managed uncommonly decent leather
brogues that toe-curl a bit, an Italian smile
intimating heat and lust and care for craft

yes, any change of place forces up generalizations
rife and ready, and even knowing how quickly
scenes arise in the mind: lithe men, short hair
long strides, briefcases, or young artists debating
over Styrian beer and new wine spritzers the edge
of mathematical, abstract space – I know really

very little: glittering steel lines of the tram
on Ungargasse, straight under my feet
and along some sections, short grass snuggles
green against silver – earth and engineering
power-sharing – what could either say to the other
about times when heels of famous men

clacked these cobblestones: Freud's boots, how he
slipped into leather smoothly pleased with strength,
and Hitler's shoes, paint bespattered, then further back
and further back again until an Ottoman stands
outside the ringed wall of the city, 300 cannon strong
the story goes, Grand Vizier Pasha tapping
his magnificent Asian slippers on these stones

PASSPORT . . .

inspected and stamped, leads to
towers and gargoyles – and cafés
the ruined faces of fathers
wide, haughty mouths of mothers
their children oblivious
except to couples
kissing on stone bridges
an old man crossing himself
as he bicycles past a cathedral

document made to bend
though not in the eyes of the law
a young woman looks at me
frankly, then waves me on
to empty my pockets, remove
my belt and pass beep-free
through their ultra-machine
these open-faced beings
the way they gaze

the pale madonnas awaiting me
lean to the left, ear touching
the baby's head, he so finely
detailed, as if Florentine artists
wanted to paint more of their power
into him than into her:
his divine versus her blessed

how her near-blandness recalls
the manner of those calm guards!
upright in blue shirts
watching at entryways
a touch of knowledge
dusting their cheeks

TRAIN RIDE

passing through Linz I notice trains
preternaturally, not the cylinders
for carrying acid chemicals
graffiti on their bulging sides
but older blocky types
of faded wood now silenced
on a weedy siding, while I sit in the upper
section, aware of speed and efficiency

across from me two young men gaze
into a camera steadied by the über-clean
hands of the blond one, occasionally
speaking quiet German phrases
while the old man cross-aisle snorts
as he sleeps though his jaw remains firm
and never once does his mouth fall slack
to reveal a vacuity no one has to see
while *I* see how I've travelled beyond
the two paragons but haven't yet arrived
at the one who catches his escaping breath
though I also note he's mastered not
sliding on his seat into a heap of age

I turn away from humans close at hand
to look again at boxcars and wonder
what they were filled with, carried
and left behind: routine stuff of light
bulbs and oddments from elsewhere
tractor parts and toiletries, nothing worse
can be imagined today as our train passes
through Linz, bearing me, grateful for
considerate and sleeping companions, easy
to say now we're going somewhere safe

TRAVELLING WITHOUT EARPLUGS

spotted cows on pasture slopes
moo where upper alpine snow
leaks into June-fed creeks constrained
in narrow rock walls, each unmoved
by burgeoning white

when evening arrives, all noises
cease here in my *pension*
except for one: someone's
far-off singing, perceptible
only when other sounds
subside, its pitch insisting
my tired mind identify
and end its *e-e-e* at once

and failing to do so
I resort to pillow-wrapping
my head, to await any dream
wherein I escape that timbre
not unlike the one (I begin to think)
we hear just before dying: such
thoughts entangle the traveller
unwisely travelling earplug-less

and who is vexed to discover
next morning the mosquito buzz
arises from the radio at his bedside
an opera-broadcasting station
not turned completely off
as if the previous person here
had been malignly planning ahead
to effect another's discomfort

and thus he suffers because he assumes
he can never correct creation
believing glumly the arrow
of the irreparable always aims for him

yet in the cool of the next dawn
he's enchanted to encounter birds
new to him singing in Italian

ON THE OCCASION OF VISITING AUDEN'S GRAVE

somehow I don't expect sighing evergreens
or cruel April's birds tuning up their notes
or the autobahn's whine beyond the church's
sweet-cream-pastry-coloured plaster walls
though I recognize the iron cross and plaque
labelling the deceased as poet and man of letters
and somehow the ivy's dense entanglement
surprises me as do wilting winter pansies
on top of the small rectangle of the plot itself
(how can it hold such long, grand bones?)
and a two-pence copper coin lying atop moss
that says he is loved by someone from home
and those admirers from other lands (like me)
know better than to swipe this little token
even as I feel its melancholic foreignness
enter my thumb and vibrate with an eagerness
to claim the wrinkled poet as my own

yes, I know how men slide daily under earth
and what remains of them upside stays briefly
before it too leaves like wind or highway noise
while calamity clots nearby, one hamlet away
even as that woman in her red coat crosses
a green field, happy black terrier leaping up
to her hand, as a crow settles his wings on pale
winter stubble, and an old man in a crushed hat
posts a letter at a yellow box – and may a reply
come sooner than he expects from a grandson
he loves to praise as only a free man can praise

but likely it's a bill, what must be paid
in a certain period before penalties apply
and debts accrue and demands mount
and a day passes in which he fails to relish
this heaven-side of grass, neglects the glory
in birdsong! – and in men whose songs rise
so smoothly from their natures we forget
how both ease and fine form came to pass
out of a morning's work in the low house
with green decorative siding not far from
his grave, a domicile easy to pass by without
a murmur of wonder – though the German words
under his photo leave me squinting, envious
of those who know more than I, who knew him
as a neighbour, summer visitor to Kirchstetten
on a back road bordered by willows ready to bud
from soggy forest floor with leaves faint for now

in Duino

narrow roads off the autobahn
offer tour buses no place to park
should passengers want
to see where Rilke slept
Princess della Torre e Tasso's gilded
family portraits of past aristocrats
staring down, uncomprehending

I step onto a balcony overlooking
the Gulf of Trieste, notice no angels
though commercial oyster beds
at the mouth of the Isonzo River
provide a symmetry the poet
may have admired from his cliff path
I am thinking a trace of gravitas
might remain on this stone
balustrade he may have touched
(or pounded) and where
in three languages is written
on its limestone lip the command
not to lean over, which I heed

Apollo beams down to warm
my thoughts again, so once more
I wonder how the poet saw from here
'wind full of cosmic space'
what remains for me white cliffs
and blue sea, curve of the gulf
and sunlight calling one wave
to appear just as another dips and
disappears without any 'endlessly
anxious hands' framing
what cannot so easily pass away

Nicholas Lanier, 1628, by Anton van Dyck

his long nose and wary look, cocked
right elbow, left hand casual on a rapier
poking back from the sparkle on its hilt
and the brightest mark? his wide forehead
below an abrupt line where brown curls
shine and announce pride, head's width
of blue sky softly clouded, sun-streak burning
above a background of fake ruins
and the focus? Lanier's lips, straight and stern
ready to sneer, yet showing beneath refinement
how many times he has been bruised
(note the hint of green at the left temple)
hairs on his red moustache curving up above
his pointed beard ready and set to quiver

he sat seven days for van Dyck, and both
clearly relished that wide swath of rich cape
tumbling down from his left and out of which
bulge his arms in red-striped fabric
such a pleasure to paint that the artist
could manage in an afternoon, highlights
of folds easy compared to the eyes some
call cold, others unarmed, the gift of art
to reflect and reveal each viewer accurately

COMMEMORATIVE ROOMS

Georg Trakl (February 3, 1887, Salzburg to November 3, 1914, Kraków)

not a word in English, yet I understand
yellowing paper holds up faded words
small books plain in design
black and white photographs
light from windows muted (a storm
is building, and later its mountain
violence breaks and drenches
my T-shirt: Salzburg, it says)
from in here I can almost see
the school he attended, still severe
and grand and yet submitting
in this city of churches, it is functional
first and only with time dignified
and perhaps saddened
that many were dead

in the short film a man's voice
intones his poems so tenderly
I am reminded that language
this harsh can be loving – because
back home we'd read translations
but never softly: scenes of the Eastern Front
required at least a twisting
of the jaw so out would come

how he himself may have sounded
gurgling on his deathbed from
an overdose of cocaine, unclear
whether suicide or error
– but forever clear his small
self-portrait: a painted darkness
of reddish hair, green face
makes a mask so unlike
the blond young man in striped trousers
seen sitting, eager not for war
but for his life – and I see
how summer light comes in
and tries its best to tell me
not to believe this possessed glow
here on the wall set to trigger
my dismay but instead to step
back into the street, where
he'd walked, shadows from clouds
falling on him as they fall on me
with sudden heat and thunder –
and did he hear in that rumble
guns that ended more
than an empire swept away
with his twenty-seven years?

what *I* hear has by now
been returned to nature, and I know
enough of this timelessness
spreads ahead, so I continue still
to look upward at stone walls
grateful they had been there
to hear a schoolboy singing

GOETHE, RINGSTRASSE

your green mantle of bronze
rose up on a street new to me
dazed me: this chance wander
and encounter! in my half-
hope to find an age not yet
complete, I saw your girth
x times larger than in real life
but what's a statue for
if not to magnify, focus, inflate?
and felt unnerved, until I spotted
the double row of buttons marching up
how classically draped your coat
how sturdy your boots, casual
drooping of your hands, your air of
certainty and even, yes, touch of
chagrin at becoming this . . .
immovable icon

earlier I'd passed towering Handel
(or was it Haydn?) I can hardly recall
now you and I are familiar: my third
(or is it fourth?) journey to remove
broken green bottle bits from
the base of your pedestal, its one
word, your name, raised in caps
I ignore traffic swelling behind us
pulse and drone of Mercedes buses
touring among snappy winds this place
has faced since long before you became
yourself, dispensing clarity as if
it were the simplest of languages

more and more you look all inward
as I gaze up, a ritual in which
I've had my umbrella blown out
by wind driving rain, same angle
I felt as a child, and I marvel
standing here, that I am able still
to find a hero in your travelling
toward Italy, in a polymath's
colours, plants – old cosmos
streamed through your mind, alchemized –
arrogance dropped, dross you spun
for us into wise gold, your face here
forever stained from rain running
to catch your down-turned lips
and I wonder if all alloyed eyes
stare into past worlds with such doubt

Galileo . . .

lived on this street, so says
a tall handsome woman
whose apartment I'm renting
one thousand years old
with modern plumbing
and beams so huge I think of
Pacific coast giants

I look across the narrow way
of Costa dei Magnoli to where
a church waits with fresh flowers
under a fading madonna's smile
when I open wide the window

and then walk out, locate his home
and high in a circle, his bearded face
a Pisces with Leo rising
hard to see, just another pale
fresco, yet strength to outlast
generations who trudged
this slope back to when
the nearby city wall held
against enemy knives

and where now I meander
pushing up along the stones
May grass high and red with
poppies as if from shed blood
and also a fragrance I catch
and fail to identify until at last
I see small dangling lemons
not quite globes, not quite suns
and think of starry ideas, just begun
his, all earth-changing, my own

no bigger than a brain's sphere
or a handful of this warm soil
to sail home with
onto a cold coast
no new moons to discover there
no orbs to name even as the lenses
I look through rearrange me
daily from fuzzy to clear
in case a heaven swims by

PUSHING TOWARD THE ALPS

I can't believe they will open and reveal
passes because from an hour away
though cloud-speckled and so
somehow soft, they're a wall
we keep driving toward, Volvo
unperturbed by the road rising
to where limestone breaks and piles
and leaves white points in the sky
summits subject to the *whap*
of a climber's ice axe far above rivers
we roll across, their gravel bottoms
almost white, scoured by rushes
of glacial flood while mountain light
slants into an evening's yellow
and shadows elongate for dusk
as a buttery castle floats past

these peaks remain unfazed
even by Zeus-fuelled lightning bolts
as if their true trick is not to think
not to have any apparatus with which
to think, their solid fame and
eye-glad beauty never knowing
that one who passes below is visited
by the flash of a former motoring
(with frayed parents that Sunday)
buried under massing decades and
arriving with a pang, alive like rain
fleeing the windshield

in Kapfenstein

in Schloss Kapfenstein I discover I have forgotten
how to dance – at my daughter's wedding
under the portrait of a long-nosed Austrian
in blue silk, descendant of Turk fighters
I stumble and step on delicate feet: three women
attempt to lead, and fail, though we enjoy anyway our
pleasure at arms up not in time with lederhosen music

and along the Danube, I find bewilderingly
I have forgotten how to ride a bike, wobbling
wildly, almost running into ambulatory tourists
and those other trim walkers from nearby vineyards
stepping along, catching breezes, in this particular
incarnation watching barges bearing down
under black, red, gold faded German flags

what everyone says cannot be forgotten
I forget and blame being unbalanced on
the hammer of intercontinental flight but know
somehow it's otherwise, as in the dream
night before the wedding: fighting off men
with moustaches and crowbars who are breaking
glass walls of my house, one man among them
attaching explosives so no hope remains
of driving him off when he turns to me and says
'Why are you so invested in this structure?'

or perhaps more like the dream the night
following, having passed through a father's tears
and into another beginning, when I am hoeing, really
cutting the ground, gruelling work, and then
an even greater effort is required: to wear
a bulky x-ray unit strapped to my chest so everyone
sees what I am feeling, that I've worked hard
at becoming soft with rewards of love's
continuance, joy's release

DISLOCATION

child takes the hand of an older brother
leads him into a house where kind-faced
violinist reaches his instrument down
and before the two boys begin
to sing to his vibrato, the child
turns back to remaining
family members clustered outside
tells them to ready their hankies
so sweet will be the music made
for the father, for whom especially
these songs are sung
            my own damp
pillow awakens me in a foreign bed
where I wonder if this dream
arrives only in dislocation, to uncover
how a constancy remains
and requires thought
so that, here, closer to the village
of my forefathers, its dust
might enter me
            on this table
peonies eager to open and bless me
with their cut dying – they might have
in incarnations of earlier seeds
graced a meal when my father's father
came home weary
found his family singing not hymns
but rhyming paeans even the youngest
knew were both his own and everyone's

OUR COMMON DUST

LOVEMAKING IN VIENNA

August night so heavy with damp
all exhaled breaths from the dead
in the Danube are falling upon the city
soggy and hot, and I throw open
casements and hope the famous *Föhn*
with its hint of pinewoods will find me
but it does not, I am too hemmed in:
tall stucco walls, windows overlooking a small
courtyard full of green feathery treetops
climbing up in moonlight – and so later
a woman's moaning slides across the leaves
close by, uninterrupted queen of the night
and I'm waking and not waking but awake enough
to wonder out of which window does love fly

and later still, when silence returns, I'm fully
attentive to hearing it, no traffic beyond my bed
to deflect or ignore
                    – and then we're all
drowsy beyond sad dreams, spines feeling
rare breeze so welcome on wet flesh
that wakefulness grows almost into desire
though sleep is strong and best

ON FIRST HEARING MAHLER'S FIFTH

first violin throws her blond braid
severely down, then up as if to knock
second violin out of tune, as if possessed
by torrents of rising and falling, mellow and unmelodic
depths that vanish into ears of listeners where nests of
feelings up till then half noted (half unwanted)
fill with formless murmurs from a forgotten life of fury

were I given a chance, a second chance, it is not
her I'd want to be, nor the popinjay-conductor
who kisses her hand held high as her head, nor even
Mahler with his face full of rivulets and futures even he
could not foretell, he with his star in the sidewalk
outside the opera house, but rather let me be
the percussionist who sits serenely
hands in his lap, cymbals tucked away in slots
until slowly he rises, pulls out the glowing alloy discs
crouches slightly, feet placed apart
for grip, legs like a wishbone, hurls his
hands together in a whammo *khurshliiiing!*
finishes by opening cymbals upward, mouths
lifted high to eat all other sounds

then he subsides into a kind of sleeping
waiting for the moment he is called upon again
to bring forth a perfect punctuation, an exclamation
for which oboe and French horn, string bass and bassoon
have been mere prelude, his the culmination
of the kind a boy-child makes when in an alley
he clangs the lids of the garbage cans, and above him
a fat matron yells down from overlooking window
into inner courtyard, Italian, German, Dutch
message always the same, to halt, to which the juvenile
replies with one more reverberation rising upward unstoppably
over all commands, obliteration that brings
primal, cup-ringing delight, his heraldic shields
victorious over adulthood's demands for quietness
out of which nothing worthwhile has yet been rung

WINDING STONE STAIRS, FLORENCE CATHEDRAL

I start on the 463 steps up
to reach the church dome
in the tight space of this vertical
tunnel and, in weak light, bent back
against the wall in a breadth intended
for one monk only
I pause with strangers
as other strangers pass earthward
their traffic so close our clothes reach out
as if to touch, even if
sweaty, and here I remember
while buying the ticket far below
that sign: 'This height not for those
with heart disease'

on the walls, a recurring notice:
'Do not write on the walls'
covered with names, not a desecration
more an understanding that
Guido and Alessandro are joining
the celebration this building is making
their rough signatures just two
of the many I pass
an international explosion of names

one pink man bending
and gasping, and we push past him
up onto the outer ledge
fresh air at an eerie height
I dare not look at those ants
on the streets, plus I feel again
that urge only satisfied by falling
so I follow the steps back in
past the stone curve untouched
for centuries, its power intact

on gangplanks, we enter the dome
greeted by giant frescoes of hell
devils' red mouths roughly painted
but so high above the worshippers' floor
they cohere, reminders that thousands
for hundreds of years
feared, turning quickly to find
faces, robes, clouds
of their sunlit saints

holds high a wand or staff
tufted with yellow ribbon
so followers can spy her flag
each group an ectoplasm
that forms and bubbles around
nuclear leader who directs all
to see what cannot be seen:
underlay of history burnt off
by sun and sea breeze, her
rapid-fire iteration of details
they can't find on their own
eyes blurred by overload

I watch always for the one
who strays away, pulled toward
sea or street ephemera as if
he can only connect
when silence surrounds him
not mob hubbub pierced by
shrill voice in charge

I want to walk beside this
wanderer, tell him to plunge
down narrow streets, go blank
in plazas, feel panic rising
to be so alone, without
a language and without a sign
except for dog-peed corners
church bells, gathering
crones and a few old men

familiars he grows fond of
when he sits on a quiet bench
as one who wears the momentary
mantle of local garb, his hands
though, still holding pamphlets

and does he remember then
the guide's arm, how it must ache
in the evening, and how her voice
croaks when she speaks to
her lover of her clever phrases
intended to inspire but flattened
made dull by day-after-day delivery
that erodes pride of place and
hollows out where breath comes from?

Albrecht Dürer and me

at the Albertina Museum

his entire life he thought
of death approaching
it was the century syphilis arrived
1500 meant the end of time
one self-portrait an imitation
of Christ

for me, it's his rabbit
each ear bent differently, every
whisker visible
its mood pensive
another sort of portrait

and his monogram –
AD, 1502 (same year
his medieval father died) –
floats beneath the brown foot
as I float

back to rodents I snared
in a winter garden
frozen next day
and still the fur soft
(or back to fuzzy lucky
charms on key rings
among coins in pockets
of the slightly odd)

from him almost all
German art springs, begins
from me up pops this poem
when here I stand
(wanting to touch the painting
and feel the fur again)
one of many awed viewers
this young hare has seen
in five centuries
even as he draws into
the calm before trembling
to ponder his animal thought

and from my departing train
I see him once more
a tall buck alert in rows
of early corn, escaped, free of
any frame – though red dots
of waving wild poppies
defining the farmer's field
draw my eye to his readiness
for leaping

Self-Portrait Nude

I stand in front of a tortured portrait
completed in 1910 by Egon Schiele:
skin reddish and raw, a scraped skeletal self
tilting, electrified by jagged outline of light
eyes closed, hair livid red blue
elsewhere in this museum
hang works of his other distortions
in legs and torso, some kink of the inner
made visible, along with the more famous
Gustav Klimts though they
failed to hold me as did these hysterical shapes
which perhaps foreshadow the artist's death by
Spanish flu, 1918, thousands dying contorted

and now I recall my father also suffered that
influenza in Detroit where he went to work
in car factories, he and his brother for days
sick in their room, young men – and
did he know they might be dying, waiting
and praying, no doubt they were praying, and
though he believed in the strength of that power
he could not deny the virus, illness eating
in him so he coughed himself up – and still
he did survive, crept out of that stinking house
an emaciated, gaunt adolescent, made
his way back to Canada to live and eventually
make me
        and I think now some spirit of Egon flew
from Vienna, drawn to my weakened father
who in his fatigue raised an arm above
his burning forehead and deflected it, returning
to himself as he was before he descended
into days of half breathing, half living with death
– and yet part of the painter entered Father
as an unseen arrow that pierced through
matter and was itself released in his last

offspring, so here I stand in this Viennese vault
recognizing myself in these twisting limbs

and later buying a black T-shirt with one of his
signature figures of skewed appendages stencilled
in shiny blue, I almost wish I hadn't succumbed
to such tourist delirium, but I needed an emblem
to remember my long-gone juvenescent wild skin
and jutting bones, my imprisoning self-pity

to evoke him, to keep him close, talisman
to protect me from my own age's plagues
coming from outside on the wind and those
eventualities from within rising up in blood
and phlegm, ushered along by semen and soul

I knock on Thomas Bernhard's door. . .

Thomas Bernhard (February 9, 1931, Herleen, Netherlands to February 12, 1989, Gmunden, Austria)

once, twice, raise the iron ring
and bring it down hard in case
his ghost is sleeping, boom
rolling over a table of books
the farmhouse locked, unattended
I can't enter the place
he called his writing prison
only half affectionately – he hated
his country if not this house
its gangly flowers' unfamiliar
pungent scent around me
as I peer in, leaning against
stone and mortar wall, brown
board, field of cut green hay
nearby, the road-edge battle
of weeds versus wheels

that hollow knocking
echoes some hollow in me
and later I read: 'I am one
of those people who cannot bear
to be anywhere and are happy only
between places,' and I think of those sought
and left behind by brown boots
the brochure depicts for walking
(*gehen denken*: going thinking)
across Alps I imagined
but stalled now, stuck
here only – and I leave then –

on to Vienna, its blindness
he railed against, its equestrian icons
I slip past, determined to go
light-footed among graves, cafés
monuments, even to him
Nestbeschmutzer, my smile
not quite that
of an innocent
book under my arm slipping
narrow street rising up:
horse droppings and
iron rims on yesteryear carriages
scraping on stone through an ageless crowd
of foreign wanderers, most unaware
Bernhard's hammer hangs
over the city, poised to fall
with a hard clanging all must hear
his joy deemed untranslatable
though still sufficient, wondrously so
for the seeker

SUN-FILLED PHOTO, DUBROVNIK. . .

where a woman laughs
says she lost 50 kilos
from the Serb shelling
– she refused to enter
the fortress, willing instead
to die in her bed

and her husband recalls
a grandmother cautioning
about the placing of money
the grandfather exclaiming
'Austria cannot lose!'
– sure as only the colonized
are sure – and betting on an empire
that ended, coin devalued

(turtles in the garden also tell
a story: when Pavo fails to feed them
on time they begin to eat the small
patch of grass they call home
either voracious or desperate)

nevertheless this terrace *is* peace:
purple blooms, cactus transplant, high
wall of stone and vine and sun-stunned
mortar, rosemary greeting at my door
to the street and its slant down
past outdoor tables and tour buses –
in Adriatic's blue and breeze (both)
where Odysseus speaks not of exile
but of travel, his messengers
minnows darting in clear sea
old woman cleaning fish at the wall
feet in lapping, evening water
three cats await her gifts
– and wet, bronzed bodies step
out of the cove into a night
already cooling around me
into a kind of home I might
remember if I stay one day more

above the Danube

we climb in heat and humidity above the Danube
and a once-upon-a-time town's constricted streets
the way up paved with slanted stone soon
a path, elevation gain severe but
breezes increase, and below becomes
picturesque as we crawl upward to ruins:
this castle held Richard the Lionheart hostage
on his homeward-bound Third Crusade
when these cream-coloured stones shone new
and the tiny space for prisoners –
iron bars across an opening in rock, a cavity
reflecting, we hope, short height then of men –
gives a chill amid August's fiercest sun

we linger on what we perceive as parapets
where others loll as well, some eager
to commune with ghosts
and at this moment we look west and discover
on a distant headland what looks like another
schloss, though not a ruin, which even at this remove
glows, its walls firm, cupolas secure, and called
we learn, the monastery of Göttweig
where Benedictines maintain themselves and
keep the sun shining as well as it does
such thoughts occur in a foreign land
where all is brightly new – and why travel if not
to grow into the unknown where we'll hit upon
what transforms us, as bread is changed
when eaten if prayers are offered beforehand
as age is held back from the listener by a story

on the way down I pick up a whitened piece
of wood or bone, hard to tell which, but certainly
weightless, and I do not believe such a thing's
a relic or a mystery or even a worthy souvenir
but for a moment I hold it, rub it close to me
thinking to link back through eras to marauders
who appeared on the river, and to villagers
who prepared wine and meat for their feast
and prayed among families after they left
that the devils would not return again before winter

in Hallstatt

red hair of the guide leads us down
into earth mined for twenty-seven centuries
though only we and our recent progenitors
are tourists, all earlier visitants came
for salt, their individual stories lost or
merged with legends from the Celt
cemetery exhumed nearby in this valley
shadowed by peaks beyond peaks and
steep walls where nothing clings but myth

had I once been one of those who wore
gold bracelets on his biceps, and if one
such prince should touch me now, will I
know, the shiver of eternal recognition
shocking me backwards out of these
protective overalls all visitors must wear
a gaggle of us turning into a platoon
in red outfits, same for me as for
the Japanese and South Africans

will I walk into these depths older than
possible to grasp, even with the dark
illuminated by the guide's torch and words
and not return to reasoning as a city-
walking, siren-cringing, magic-missing
modern but find beneath these mass clothes
bronze body armour, and in my hand the
amber-embellished hilt of an iron sword
that led me over more than mountains

later we eat fish from the crystal lake
and under the calm of local wine speak of
the last war here, of a mother who carried
to her grave hope her missing son might
yet return, and then I sleep, my femurs not
unlike those in the close-by charnel house
until its flanking church's pre-dawn bells
announce I must begin again the work
of unearthing who I might yet become

Crying in the Belvedere

young woman quite near
presses against young man
black hair dishevelled
ragged mouth twisted in tears
pushed open on his chest – is she
reseeing *The Kiss*, the way it pulsed
(so unlike kitschy postcard's gold message)
or was it Napoleon on his silver
steed, crimson cape twirling over
forward thrust of conquered soil?

did a different draft of history
creep near and enter her?
in upper rooms von Ribbentrop
forced two men from Belgrade
to capitulate, sign Axis papers
in presence of Italian and Japanese
government men supercilious
in their self-regard and disrespect
for two seized Slavs, whose people
would repudiate their signing and fight
fully knowing they must die

I look as closely as a furtive glance
allows: her luxurious hair flames,
face now not completely crumpled
though wet, shining – the man?
stares over her head into
futures not perfectly free, lips pursed
perhaps praying for rescue by
regiments under the command of
hero-warrior rewarded with
this mansion, Eugene of Savoy
whose iron statue dominates
entry to another palace safely far
from here, with other trysts

Vindobona

along the river I sniff out traces of you
of the Roman legions, emperor, philosopher-king
the term best suiting you, smell stones older
even than you, blank odour of rock
still hard and striated, rounded
not at all diminished since you arrived
with your phalanxes, here

determined to keep back un-order, a requirement
I recognize as necessary in myself although
my forebears fought against you, in the curled wood
their wild hair filled with light from gods (less rational
than yours) that you never doubted
walked among forest foes
at this place where the river bends, guards posted
at night, you writing Greek

shards of illumination that help when I wander
now by our Danube, my eye returning to
dip of wave repeating against stony shore
coming to announce an endless way like wind
among shoreline poplars, wooded hills
dropping down to water where vineyards crowd
and where across the river under the trees
once lurked a strength you pitched yourself
against, taking in its chthonic politics and fighting
for a different border between here and hereafter

FOUR WORKERS

two short women in green uniforms
cross the street with me, their talk
pleasurable in the cozy way they bend
to and from one another, dirt
on their knees as we walk past flower
patches and quivery shrubs
summer leaves wearing
clear droplet pearls

now two men in neon
orange overalls push wheelbarrows
of trash the city has offered them
both gaunt giants snarling into smoke
swirling up from lips as they scan
gutters in a silence marked by
glowering neither notices in the other
the way they talk and signal
by placing rake at an angle
amidst our common dust

A MOMENT OF

MISSING BELLS

RUGBY IN THE SEVENTEENTH DISTRICT

young men ram, thrust, brace against
one another, pass the ball backwards, kick it
high and out of bounds, squirm along
grass and stain their shorts and knees
with mud – yet how they run, ignoring
strain because of what lies ahead:
the flash of victory or (too raw to consider)
its counterpoint, a fiasco bringing tears
and incrimination in post-game review

in the stands, fans, two kinds only:
for favourite and for underdog
each with colours and erupting into
roars and monster chants though
rooters sit side by side on wooden slats
many smoking, then leaping to cheer a rush
a scrum, groaning when a critical kick
goes wide and linesman's orange flag
does not flash up to announce a triumph
and so famous local beer is downed
those tall green cans of yellow brew

that help enliven even a limp game, which this
championship is not, the golden cup waiting
medals glinting, eager to grace sweating necks
of victors – and women wave, not themselves
just now, catapulted into those who lean
out to touch heroes of the plastered hair
while ignoring around them the handsome men
though steady partners they may otherwise be
and who themselves bask in the gusto of
their fellow paladins, their sex's zest
confirmed at a remove they appreciate more
than the contact and knock admired
in the moment by their wives

ARMOURY AT GRAZ

'goose belly' they called the breastplate
that presented a 16th-century foot soldier
to his enemy as someone rich and fat
and thus a victor in any battle with mace
and halberd, and all soldiers of any side
short then, a grown man's foot
no bigger than a child's now
only horse soldiers slightly larger
each with two pistols, two shots
to pierce opposing helmeted heads
about flank height
their mounts also small and tough
though not so they would jump
rows of upraised pikes, chest level

I wander these floors of weaponry
the cannons decorated, their cannonballs
plain and larger than a schoolboy's globe
I try on a helmet and feel its weight
bend my neck, crest of grey metal
reaching up to give an ego advantage
and even an hour after I hefted a sabre
the smell of iron clings to my fingers
while smoke from front-loaders blows
and men and horses scream as they fall
on blood-and-piss-soaked earth that a duke
determines worth defending or gaining, borders
always a line no one dying could be sure of
another threshold requiring crossing instead

I come to noticing last the small windows
their original panes rippling and wavy
so I see imperfectly the world beyond
and this one so remote it holds no fear
the long-barrelled guns needing
hardly any light except what little
we might throw their way in our thinking
of what creatures we once were
and still remain in our claiming
of ground – my own country like this too
far enough away that I do not feel
its grasp upon me though I know if pressed
I would find its war-light flickering within

Anton Bruckner

the fabled musicians perform Mozart
as if it were mere play, but when they move
to Bruckner, the violinists sit up like cats
ready for lunch, first violinist
first among favourites, black hair
a heap upon a gleaming brow
raked by fingers of supple power

earlier, at intermission
the second violinist had stepped out
for a cigarette needed not for nerves
but for air outside the hall, walls
golden as the secured waves in his curls
and returning late to the stage, apologized
profusely but quietly (but profusely)
to the conductor whose sharp forgiveness
for tardiness runs through the horns
like a charge, shock
perhaps all the better (thinks
the conductor) for the Bruckner

from the second row, I admire
these working faces, the bending
and near lifting-off of backbones
from stiff chairs, and though I admit
little know-how with such sound
I hear with my heart
the undulant green landscape
the brook, near, below a bridge
roving melancholy never far
and as sometimes happens
I fall under a spell partly
of my own making and awake
only when the clapping and bravos
ignite around me, uniting us with
the magicians who beam and bow
each effortlessly convinced
that their music was intended
as its composer intended
to speak of polyphonic God

Central Cemetery

. . . we arrive at the graveyard, one of mankind's most underrated symbols of civilization.

– Josephine Hart, *The Truth About Love*

we walk through the walled place
admiring the quietness of the dead
the often tidy commemorations
of the three million who stopped here
some in crypts, or in fresh graves, a few
decorated wildly, rightly – Beethoven's
bones hum there beneath the stone
and there, someone not so famous (though
to his daughters perhaps more notable)
lid of the crypt lifted off, its iron
handles handled once more before
bones are lowered and added to an older
layer of familial skeletons waiting

meanwhile wind pushes at us
and at the trees, squirrels (one red
chasing the black) fling themselves
up trunks – it's then we enter old
Jewish grounds where 60,000 lie buried
and paths narrow, overgrown
ivy triumphing over headstones
of Hirsch and Epstein, nettles reaching out
from graves to brush our ankles
and bird calls seem to intensify
as if to compensate for what the shrunken
community cannot manage: to keep visible
these hidden markers and toppling
indicators, this jumble history's way
of leaving behind an unexpected scene

and yet how perfect an example of
what Freud (whose ashes repose not here
but in London) affirms: the animate
triumphs over the inanimate – and we
find in the amassing of grass and tendrils
a tenderness cool with natural shade
not so evident in trimmed lawns
below crosses, mounds, carefully
tended flowers brightly coloured just
across the road, closer to the centre
where a building with cement saints
and bulging green dome points up beyond
any name undergoing erasure whether etched
recently in marble or already eaten by seasons
of leaves, roots, leaves, roots, leaves

Sigmund Freud Museum . . .

I avoid and then its attraction
overcomes my aversion
and what's unconscious in me
begins to walk up Berggasse
wind blowing trash and sand
in my teeth, telling me to sidestep
into a second-hand store across
from #19, an easy diversion

then in his former rooms I watch
old home movies: his white head
wobbles, his clacking jaw says
even a giant turns frail, fails
needs a blanket over the knees
in some flower garden far from here
strong grandsons near his cane

the look-alike visitors: eager, studious
whereas I'm in the toilet wishing
I had the nerve to scrawl a joke
on white walls, one to make him laugh
but I have no marker and no
wit either, just a bit of
bratty vile-and-bile I can't express
though, believe me, I know it's there

what remains? the ratty maroon
furniture (the couch left with him
when he fled), not the Nazis
who hung their flag in his doorway
maybe some sentences, the few
I have read, but greater than these
this image of agedness: perhaps
paltry, not tattered, in tie and suit,
near enough to death to be hallowed

which grieves me, that he who said
all was drive and fatality would
himself be required to turn and face
what came next, as if I were thinking
– wildly, strangely, wrought by dust –
that someone among us might be exempt
from the final exit out of flesh
knowing of course it wouldn't be me
the one still talking, hoping for a cure

James Joyce / Italo Svevo Museum

on via Madonna del Mare
I take the stairs up to discover letters
he wrote, his daughter Lucia recording
his words though omitting the essential
recovered: 'I am dictating this, and
in English, as I have not sufficiently
from a fresh eye attack to be able to read
or write,' which draws me back
to photos of the man with his obscuring
glasses as if his imagined worlds
were of such vividness he could not
look both out and in, and the fates knew
in would be the greater view

this letter written to console
the widow of Italo Svevo, dead
nine years after a sepia print presents
him and his wife on their anniversary
(30 July 1919) watching fondly
their daughter Letizia whose husband
Antonio Fonda Savio gazes at his
beloved, and she broadly smiling
in her receiving of pure adoration

on my way down the steps to the street
a student comes up, frowning, occupied
by his worries, not quite seeing
though we manage not to collide
and something of *his* blindness comes
into me, I grasp he is wanting
to fill the holes he feels, or perhaps
he desires a brother to rescue him
the way Stanislaus helped James
before war tore Trieste beyond aid

later in another nearby museum I
stare at Greek statuary and reflect how time
is tough on noses, each one here broken or
shattered, how sad these features appear
staring from blank eyes, and I am grateful
that photographs and phrases bring me close
allow my eye and imagination to believe in life
even if some pieces now and then are missing

DEPARTURE AND RETURN

1. departure

you do not want to leave, to step out the door
after saying goodbye to those who remain
inside, already returning to their lives, cleaning
away what you have left behind and thinking
soon their daily routine will re-establish
in the arc forward into the day after you
pulled your suitcase over their threshold in
a clatter of wheels ushering you to the cab
and on to the airport where you fall into that
being-blank world, herds hauling themselves
home or away, exiting excited or exhausted

and having left behind loved ones, you
accept the return to the silence of your rooms
their hush, no one exclaiming over a doodad
found in a shop, held, tossed and finally bought
with money of a different colour from the kind
now in your wallet, and no one to step inside
the circle of your arms, someone who easily
holds you back from drifting into a trance
whose edges are sharper than the sound of
your key turning in the door, your nose
taking in days not spent here and where
you need to return, first by opening
windows and then by unzipping luggage
and letting their ghosts escape to haunt you
momentarily until you shower and sleep

dream raggedly, incomprehensibly the same
as you dreamt in far places where you went
to become someone other than yourself, a
surprisingly easy enough adventure you might
someday repeat once home has become again
the place you love enough to leave behind
its comforts growing around you until you
fling them back into dusty corners and
light out to where your eye gets fed on
a stone bridge, view of a lake, streets full
of strangers walking past, not seeing you –
the one you might attempt in that new air

2. return: young woman from Sarajevo

seatmate on the flight home has
rumpled hair back of her head, as do
all of us who travel on the long-sleep haul

our bodies struggling gracelessly with so much
stimulation, and we talk very little, too aware
of need for conserving energy in ourselves

but I glimpse her passport with its harsh American
eagle and note the way she smiles when I open
Crankshaw's *The Fall of the House of Habsburg*

and so I learn her husband is Bosnian and
will be travelling later from his homeland to join her
in Sioux Falls (a city I struggle to fix to a state)

and I think briefly of speaking of my surprise
at seeing fresh flowers on the coffin of Emperor
Franz Joseph (uncle to 'suspicious, misanthropic'

doomed Archduke Franz Ferdinand) in Vienna's
underground *Kapuzinergruft,* but restrain my questions
and when we stand later in the aisle after landing

both eager to breathe new air, I say her husband
will be asleep by now, past midnight his time
while we flew on through endless light

she wishes me good luck and touches the back of
my hand where it rests on top of a seat, a sincere
gesture but also one hinting I might need help

crossing nearly half the globe today, or perhaps
she's returning a kindness for mentioning her spouse
whom she left at dawn, knowing then his time zone

was not just Sarajevo's with its honours
of horrors and beauty but also that realm
everyone occasionally, reluctantly leaves

3. return: arriving from Munich

in Chicago I am told the truth:
I have missed my connecting flight

thereafter, chaos: waves of travellers
their carts and suitcases merging, bewildered

by fat, black woman's tone of command
– for what had they done wrong but land

in ORD, stunned by physical onslaught
of chasing the sun, and the monitor tells all

to each of us whether bound for Omaha, Orlando
or Kansas City or not, shining blue and white

in tiny type, a wall no one goes to, fearing to cross
the line troglodytic men make as they flip

monster suitcases onto conveyor belts
their beer bellies in no way diminishing

their strength, taking my personal misfortune
as a given, not worth talking about

and baby held ahead of me begins to cry
her mother in head scarf, her father unremarkable

except that he's leading them into
a new life, in Dallas, that name in history

they cannot really claim as theirs though today
we have all seen guns at passport control

that make us long for homelands temporarily
unattainable, or already left behind

4. return: oval window

a portal like no other
looks down into forest-top
clouds puffy or matte grey
constant sword-length
cutting across, wobbling
so it's wise to fall away
from thrum of the actual, dome
blue-black above, the sickening tilt

and see instead remembered swifts squeaking
wheeling over parapets of castle stone
where brave men died in previous years
meeting firepower at dawn or from damp

man speaking Polish
sneezes, brings me back to
not earth but its high-flying
flight attendant's steely smile
Dutch woman chiding
my lack of savvy: to travel
without a pen
for customs form
ballpoint she disdains to take back
when I exit – such a stance

after all my successful
ignoring of thirty thousand feet
weight of luggage and imaginings
so earth passes below more serenely
than ever felt when dropped in on

5. return: over snow

flying home from far away
jets seem to stall
I'm thankful to find
at last
my country below
features we otherwise call
white, grey and black
not one sign of humankind

there lies snow upon snow, soft
from this height
or a peak protrudes
white slashes its face
what might live there
long swept away: home
somehow, space without provenance

its relief lets me relinquish
cities with fables
and five more airborne hours
traversing tundra and taiga
before gaining my bed

that still point found on no map
but mine, its welcome
now absurdly foreign, alien
as once was last night's European bolster

WEEDS GREW WHILE I WAS AWAY

I expected what?
an unchanged patch
of pure stasis, stems
unaltered, exactly as
the morning I glanced back
from the cab, my face sunny
not this yellow of greeters
trumpeting on my lawn
crowding the walk where birds
splatter white words
around the grey face
of the garden stone
that has not altered, cool
under my hand, a spot more
lichen-wrinkle persisting

– that this filigree lives
so little, unlike the rise
and fall we are made of
we hardly care, so pleased
we alone measure how slow
rock crumbles, as we touch it
we rub against time and find
we triumph: listen
to our watery laughter
when sun lights up skin
we have animal pleasure
knowing and loving
even ragweeds with their vigour
and niche so like our own
in urgencies coming and going

A MOMENT OF MISSING BELLS

on a construction site, a crowbar falls on a pail
at such an angle that metal on metal rings out
to the plaza where I sit near mumbling fountains
half in shadow, half in sun, in view of distant water
and I twist my head to catch the sound again

as if a bell *has* rung, and in that instant I walk again
in Wien amidst the pealing, air-filling, calling chimes
resounding out from corner churches, sending their
iron-made messages of attention and intent
through pedestrians hurrying to destinations of

torte trysts, formal assignations or sitting alone
with tiny porcelain cups in hand, which tremble
in sympathetic vibration, and so the big and
little are joined as the hourly resonance
floats over the city, causes its denizens to

gaze upward at spires and to imagine themselves
ascending, asking how it feels to have ascension
inside them, a tintinnabulation growing, climbing out
of one's chest since first burst of the clapper striking
told how a small tick has been carved out of time

Notes

The first quotation in 'In Duino' is taken from the first of Rilke's elegies in *The Essential Rilke,* selected and translated by Galway Kinnell and Hannah Liebmann. The second quotation is also from Rilke's first elegy and is taken from *Selected Poems, Rilke,* translated by J.B. Leishman.

The quotation in 'I knock on Thomas Bernhard's door' is from *Wittgenstein's Nephew* by Thomas Bernhard, translated by David McLintock.

'Vindobona' was the name of the Roman settlement where Vienna now stands, and where Marcus Aurelius died at the age of fifty-eight on March 17, 180 of an infectious disease. His last words were 'Weep not for me, think rather of the pestilence and the deaths of so many others.'

Acknowledgements

Some poems, some in earlier versions, appeared in *Event, The Malahat Review, The Windsor Review* and in the anthologies *Poet to Poet* (Guernica, 2012) and *Best Canadian Poetry in English 2013* (Tightrope Books, 2013).

Special thanks to those who read various versions: Robert Adams, gillian harding-russell, Lorna McCallum, Meg Stainsby, Richard Therrien and Russell Thornton.

Special thanks also to Silas White and to Kurt Klima.

Photo by Margery Patrick

About the Author

David Zieroth has published several books of poetry including *The Fly in Autumn*, which won the Governor General's Literary Award for Poetry, and *How I Joined Humanity at Last*, which won the Dorothy Livesay Poetry Prize. He taught at Douglas College in New Westminster, BC, before retiring and founding The Alfred Gustav Press. Born in Neepawa, Manitoba, he lives in North Vancouver, BC.